Mom-Preneurship Made Easy: 5 Business Ideas Under $100

Introduction:

In the hustle and bustle of daily life, many moms find themselves juggling numerous responsibilities, from managing households and caring for their families to pursuing personal passions and dreams. But what if we told you that you can embark on a thrilling journey of entrepreneurship without breaking the bank? Yes, it's true – welcome to the world of mom-preneurs!

"Moms are natural problem-solvers, multi-taskers, and creators, making them perfect candidates for starting their own businesses."

In this book, "Mom-preneurs: 5 Business Ideas to Start with $100," we invite you to explore a realm of possibilities where moms from all walks of life are transforming their dreams into reality. Armed with just $100 and an abundance of creativity, these resilient women have carved out their niches in the world of business, and they are here to inspire you to do the same.

Throughout the following chapters, we will delve into five incredible business ideas that require minimal initial investment but offer unlimited potential for growth and fulfillment. Whether you're a stay-at-home mom looking to generate income from the comfort of your living room or a working mom seeking a flexible venture that complements your existing job, there's a business idea within these pages that's tailor-made for you.

Our journey begins with the allure of "Handmade Crafts and Jewelry." Discover how moms like you are tapping into their artistic flair to craft unique creations that capture the hearts of customers worldwide. From sourcing affordable materials to marketing your handmade wonders, we'll guide you through every step of the creative process.

Next, we unveil the magic of "Personalized Gift Baskets." Gone are the days of generic gifts – moms are now curating personalized baskets that bring joy and meaning to every occasion. Learn how to assemble eye-catching gift sets on a budget and turn your passion for gifting into a rewarding enterprise.

If you have a green thumb and a love for nature, the "Plant Nursery" chapter is sure to pique your interest. Embrace the flourishing world of gardening and discover the secrets to nurturing plants and cultivating a thriving plant nursery business, all while contributing to a greener, more sustainable future.

"Pet Services" are on the rise as more and more pet owners seek reliable and caring services for their furry companions. In this chapter, we explore how moms are combining their affection for animals with an entrepreneurial spirit to offer dog walking, pet sitting, and grooming services that enrich the lives of both pets and their owners.

Last, but not least, the "Subscription Box Service" trend has taken the e-commerce world by storm. We'll introduce you to moms who have tapped into this exciting market, delighting subscribers with curated boxes of joy month after month.

So, if you're ready to embark on an empowering journey that blends motherhood with entrepreneurship, turn the page and let the adventure begin. You possess all the ingenuity, resourcefulness, and determination needed to succeed as a mom-preneur.

Let's unlock your potential and celebrate the beauty of balancing family and business as we explore these five business ideas, each enriched with real-life stories and practical advice.

Get ready to embrace your role as a mom-preneur, where passion meets profit, creativity finds its canvas, and dreams blossom into reality. Your journey to business success starts now!

Chapter 1: Handmade Crafts and Jewelry

Explore the Appeal of Handmade Crafts and Jewelry in Today's Market

In a world of mass-produced goods and automated manufacturing, there is a growing allure and appreciation for the personal touch and

uniqueness that come with handmade crafts and jewelry. As consumers seek authentic and meaningful connections with the products they buy, the market for artisanal creations has witnessed a remarkable resurgence. In this article, we delve into the reasons behind the enduring appeal of handmade crafts and jewelry and how they continue to captivate hearts and minds in today's fast-paced marketplace.

Crafting Artistry and Uniqueness

Handmade crafts and jewelry embody the essence of artistry and individuality. Each piece is crafted with passion, skill, and attention to detail, making it a tangible expression of the creator's artistic vision. Unlike mass-produced items that come off assembly lines, handmade products exude a distinct charm and character that can't be replicated. They tell a story of the artisan's creative journey and are a celebration of human ingenuity and craftsmanship.

Embracing Sustainability and Ethical Consumption

The rising consciousness of environmental impact and ethical consumption has driven more consumers to seek alternatives to products with questionable origins. Handmade crafts and jewelry often boast sustainable sourcing, eco-friendly materials, and responsible production practices. Artisans are inclined to prioritize quality over quantity, leading to reduced waste and a lower carbon footprint. By supporting handmade, consumers can align their values with their purchases and contribute to a more sustainable future.

Fostering Community and Connection

Beyond the tangible aspects of the products themselves, the handmade movement fosters a sense of community and connection between artisans and consumers. Customers who buy handmade items often cherish the personal connection with the creators, establishing a bond that transcends a mere buyer-seller relationship. Artisan markets, craft fairs, and online platforms provide a space for artists and crafters to interact directly with their customers, sharing stories, inspiration, and insights into their creative process.

Preserving Heritage and Cultural Traditions

Handmade crafts and jewelry are often steeped in cultural heritage and traditions, reflecting a rich history that spans generations. Artisans often draw inspiration from their cultural roots, infusing their work with elements of folklore, symbolism, and time-honored techniques. By embracing handmade products, consumers become patrons of cultural preservation, supporting the continuity of traditional craftsmanship and artistic expressions that might otherwise fade away.

Unveiling the "Human Element"

Amidst the digital era's efficiency and automation, handmade crafts and jewelry offer what some have termed the "human element." Purchasing a handmade item is not just buying a physical object but investing in the story and passion behind it. It allows consumers to connect with the makers, understanding their dreams and dedication. This sense of involvement, appreciation, and authenticity resonates with people seeking more meaningful and mindful consumption experiences.

Step-by-Step Guide to Starting a Handmade Crafts and Jewelry Business

Starting a handmade crafts and jewelry business can be an exciting and fulfilling venture. Here's a step-by-step guide to help you launch your creative enterprise successfully:

Step 1: Define Your Niche and Target Market

Determine the type of crafts and jewelry you want to create. Focus on your passions and strengths to find a niche that sets you apart.

Identify your target market. Understand their preferences, style, and price range to tailor your designs to meet their needs.

Step 2: Research and Plan

Conduct market research to identify trends, competitors, and pricing strategies within your niche.

Create a business plan outlining your goals, marketing strategies, budget, and sales projections.

Step 3: Source High-Quality Materials

Look for reputable suppliers that offer a wide range of quality materials for your crafts and jewelry.

Consider buying materials in bulk to secure discounts and reduce costs.

Step 4: Develop Unique Designs

Let your creativity flow and create designs that reflect your artistic vision and cater to your target market's preferences.

Experiment with various materials and techniques to add uniqueness to your products.

Step 5: Build Your Brand Identity

Choose a brand name and design a captivating logo that represents your style and vision.

Create a cohesive brand image across your products, packaging, and marketing materials.

Step 6: Set Up Your Workshop

Designate a space in your home or rent a studio where you can create your crafts and jewelry comfortably.

Organize your workspace to optimize efficiency and creativity.

Step 7: Create Sample Products

Develop a collection of sample products that showcase the diversity of your crafts and jewelry designs.

Use these samples for product photography and promotional materials.

Step 8: Pricing Strategies

Calculate the cost of materials, labor, and overhead expenses to determine the base cost of each product.

Set your pricing based on market research, competitor analysis, and perceived value. Ensure your prices are competitive yet profitable.

Step 9: Brand Your Packaging

Create attractive and professional packaging that enhances the perceived value of your crafts and jewelry.

Add branding elements like labels, tags, or business cards to create a lasting impression.

Step 10: Establish an Online Presence

Create a website or set up a shop on popular online platforms like Etsy or Shopify to showcase and sell your products.

Use professional-quality photographs and compelling product descriptions to entice potential customers.

Step 11: Market Your Business

Utilize social media platforms to build a following and engage with your target audience. (I favor Instagram and TikTok.)

Participate in craft fairs, trade shows, and local events to showcase your products and network with potential customers and retailers.

Step 12: Focus on Customer Service

Provide exceptional customer service to build loyalty and gain positive reviews and referrals.

Address customer inquiries promptly and ensure timely delivery of orders.

You can create a brand that connects with consumers and uses your passion and creativity to brighten people's lives via your one-of-a-kind products by following these steps and putting those qualities into your handmade crafts and jewelry company.

Success Story

Success Story: A Journey of Personal Empowerment and Artistic Expression

Meet Sarah Johnson, a devoted mother of two and a talented artist who transformed her passion for crafting into a thriving handmade crafts and jewelry business. Fueled by her love for creativity and a desire to contribute to her family's financial well-being, Sarah embarked on this entrepreneurial journey with just a small investment of $100.

Sarah's dedication to sourcing high-quality materials and her eye for intricate designs set her products apart in the market. Through strategic social media marketing and participating in local craft fairs, Sarah's brand quickly gained recognition and a loyal customer base.

Amidst the craft fair's colorful chaos, I stumbled upon Sara's enchanting jewelry stall. Our eyes met, and an instant connection sparked. We bonded over our shared roles as moms and creative souls. That chance encounter blossomed into a treasured friendship, and now, as fellow mom-preneurs, we support each other's entrepreneurial dreams.

Little did I know that Sara's talent and dedication would propel her business to remarkable heights. With her unique designs captivating hearts far and wide, Sara now boasts an astounding profit of over $50,000 per month. Her resounding success stands as a testament to the power of passion and perseverance in the world of mom-preneurs. Her achievements continue to inspire me on my own journey of turning passions into purposeful ventures.

Interview with Sarah:

Q: What inspired you to start your handmade crafts and jewelry business?

Sarah: As a mom, I wanted to find a way to balance my love for art with my responsibilities at home. Starting this business not only allowed me to express myself creatively, but it also gave me a sense of personal empowerment.

Q: How did you manage to create unique designs that resonate with your customers?

Sarah: I draw inspiration from nature and the world around me. I also listen to my customers' feedback and preferences, which helps me tailor my designs to their liking.

Q: What advice would you give to other moms aspiring to start their own handmade business?

Sarah: Follow your passion and stay true to your style. Don't be afraid to take risks and embrace the learning curve. It's a journey of self-discovery and growth, and the rewards are truly gratifying.

Chapter 2: Personalized Gift Baskets

Introduction:

Giving gifts has a specific meaning in a world that frequently moves at a rapid pace. The joy of presenting a carefully curated gift that perfectly captures the recipient's preferences and personality is an experience cherished by both the giver and the receiver. As the pursuit of meaningful connections and heartfelt gestures gains momentum, the demand for personalized gift baskets has emerged as a delightful trend in the realm of gifting.

The ability to make these considerate gifts without going over budget is a great benefit hidden among the appeal of personalised gift baskets. Crafters may start an adventure of artistic curation with a little expenditure of around $100, building a special tale for each recipient without sacrificing quality or originality.

The growing popularity of personalized gift baskets has paved the way for creative entrepreneurs on a budget to shine. Assembling these thoughtful bundles has become an art form that ignites passions and fulfills a sense of purpose. Crafters and entrepreneurs alike find joy in crafting unforgettable moments for others, and with an investment of less than $100, they can embark on a fulfilling journey that celebrates both creativity and financial mindfulness.

Curating gift baskets is an art that combines creativity, thoughtfulness, and a keen understanding of the recipient's preferences. Whether it's for a special occasion, a celebration, or simply to express appreciation, the process involves creating a unique experience that leaves a lasting impression. Here's a step-by-step guide to crafting meaningful and memorable gift baskets:

Step 1: Know Your Recipient

Understand the recipient's interests, hobbies, and tastes. Tailor the contents of the gift basket to align with their preferences, ensuring that each item resonates with them on a personal level.

Step 2: Choose a Theme

Select a theme for the gift basket that ties the items together cohesively. Themes could be based on hobbies, pampering, gourmet delights, self-care, or any other idea that suits the occasion and the recipient's personality.

Step 3: Source Affordable Items

Look for affordable yet high-quality items that fit the chosen theme. Explore local stores, online marketplaces, and discount outlets to find budget-friendly options without compromising on quality.

Step 4: Create a Focal Point

Choose a standout item that serves as the centerpiece of the gift basket, capturing the essence of the theme. This focal point draws attention and sets the tone for the rest of the items.

Step 5: Complementing Elements

Add complementary items that enhance the overall theme and support the focal point. Consider including a mix of practical and indulgent treats to create a well-rounded experience.

Step 6: Appeal to the Senses

Incorporate elements that appeal to the recipient's senses. This could include scented candles, gourmet chocolates, soothing lotions, or visually appealing décor that elevates the overall aesthetic.

Step 7: Arrange Thoughtfully

Carefully arrange the items in the basket, ensuring they are visible and well-presented. Consider layering items or using tissue paper to add depth and dimension.

Step 8: Personalize with a Message

Include a heartfelt note or a personalized message to convey your sentiments and make the gift basket even more meaningful. And Here are some examples:

Example 1:

"Dear [Recipient's Name],

Wishing you a birthday filled with joy, laughter, and all the things you love. As you embark on another year of life, I've curated this special gift basket with some of your favorite things to make your day even more memorable. From the gourmet chocolates that tantalize your taste buds to the scented candle that adds a warm glow to your space, each item is a reflection of how much you mean to me. May this gift bring a smile to your face and remind you that you are cherished.

With love and best wishes,

[Your Name]"

Example 2:

"To my dearest friend,

Thank you for being an incredible source of strength and support. As a token of my gratitude, I've assembled this gift basket filled with pampering essentials to help you unwind and take some well-deserved 'me time.' The nourishing body lotion, soothing tea, and inspiring book are all chosen with your wellness in mind. You've been there for me through thick and thin, and I hope this gift brings you the same comfort and joy that you bring to my life.

With love and appreciation,

[Your Name]"

Creating Appealing Packaging: Elevating the Presentation

Packaging plays a crucial role in the overall appeal of gift baskets. It serves as the first impression and sets the tone for the recipient's experience. Here are essential tips for creating appealing packaging:

Step 1: Choose the Right Basket or Container

Select a basket or container that complements the theme and size of the gift items. Opt for attractive, reusable options that add value to the overall gift.

Step 2: Add a Touch of Creativity

Consider embellishing the packaging with ribbons, bows, or personalized tags. These small touches add an extra layer of thoughtfulness and elegance.

Step 3: Consider Wrapping or Shrink Wrapping

If the gift items are loose or need protection, consider wrapping them in clear cellophane or using shrink-wrap to maintain the presentation.

Step 4: Branding and Brand Identity

Incorporate your brand logo or personalized label on the packaging to reinforce your brand identity. This adds a professional touch and makes your gift baskets easily recognizable.

Step 5: Create a WOW Factor

Surprise the recipient by hiding a few unexpected treasures within the packaging. This element of surprise enhances the gift-giving experience.

Step 6: Attention to Detail

Ensure that the packaging is neat, tidy, and securely wrapped. Attention to detail in the presentation reflects the care and effort put into curating the gift basket.

Remember, the art of curating gift baskets and creating appealing packaging lies in striking the perfect balance between thoughtful curation, personalization, and an eye-catching presentation. By combining these elements, you can craft gift baskets that not only delight the recipient but also leave a lasting impression of your care and creativity.

Marketing Tips for Personalized Gift Baskets:

1. **Create an Online Presence**: Establish a professional website or e-commerce platform to showcase your gift baskets. Use engaging product photography and compelling product descriptions. Leverage social media platforms to reach a wider audience and engage with potential customers.
2. **Social Media Marketing**: Utilize social media to build a loyal following. Share behind-the-scenes content, customer testimonials, and sneak peeks of upcoming gift baskets. Run promotions, giveaways, and seasonal campaigns to attract more customers.

3. **Email Marketing**: Build an email subscriber list and send out regular newsletters with exclusive offers, gift ideas, and updates about your business. Personalize the content to cater to the interests of your subscribers.
4. **Collaborate with Influencers**: Partner with influencers and bloggers in your niche to showcase your gift baskets. Their endorsements can significantly increase your brand visibility and credibility.
5. **Offer Customization Options**: Highlight your ability to personalize gift baskets for any occasion. Encourage customers to share their unique gifting needs, and create bespoke solutions that resonate with them.
6. **Leverage Customer Reviews and Testimonials**: Display positive customer reviews and testimonials on your website and social media. Positive feedback builds trust and encourages potential customers to make a purchase.
7. **Seasonal and Holiday Promotion**s: Create special promotions and discounts for holidays, birthdays, anniversaries, and other occasions. Develop themed gift baskets tailored to the season or event.

Expanding Business through Special Occasions and Corporate Partnerships:

1. **Corporate Gifting Programs**: Develop corporate gifting programs targeting businesses seeking thoughtful gifts for employees, clients, or partners. Offer discounts on bulk orders and customization options to suit their branding and messaging.

2. **Weddings and Events**: Partner with wedding planners and event organizers to provide personalized gift baskets for guests or event attendees. Tailor the gifts to match the theme and atmosphere of the occasion.
3. **Collaborate with Local Businesses**: Form partnerships with local businesses, such as boutiques, florists, or spas, to cross-promote each other's products. Offer your gift baskets as add-ons or complementary gifts to their offerings.
4. **Gift Registry Services**: Introduce a gift registry service where customers can curate personalized gift baskets for their special occasions. Promote this service to engaged couples, expecting parents, and those celebrating milestones.
5. **Corporate Partnerships for Employee Incentives**: Collaborate with companies to provide personalized gift baskets as rewards for their employees' achievements or milestones. Offer a range of options to suit different preferences and occasions.
6. **Create Limited-Edition Collections**: Design limited-edition gift basket collections tied to special events, themes, or collaborations. This exclusivity can create a sense of urgency and drive more sales.
7. **Fundraising and Charity Events**: Participate in fundraising events or donate gift baskets to charity auctions. This not only raises brand awareness but also showcases your commitment to giving back to the community.

By implementing these marketing tips and exploring strategic partnerships, your personalized gift basket business can reach new heights and establish a strong presence in both special occasions and corporate gifting sectors. Always keep customer satisfaction at the core of your efforts, and continuously innovate to stay ahead in the competitive market.

Success Story : From Stay-at-Home Mom to Creative Entrepreneur

Meet Lisa Adams, a stay-at-home mom who turned her love for personalized gift-giving into a successful business venture. With a keen eye for detail and a knack for curating thoughtful gift baskets, Lisa started her personalized gift basket service with minimal capital investment.

By sourcing budget-friendly items and creatively packaging each gift basket, Lisa's brand quickly gained popularity among individuals and corporate clients alike. Her passion for making every occasion special has earned her a reputation for creating unique and heartwarming gift experiences.

Interview with Lisa:

Q: How did you identify the market need for personalized gift baskets?

Lisa: As a mom, I always enjoyed creating thoughtful gifts for my family and friends. I realized that many people were looking for personalized gift options that go beyond the typical store-bought presents.

Q: How did you manage to keep costs low while maintaining the quality of your gift baskets?

Lisa: I'm always on the lookout for affordable yet charming items to include in my baskets. By building strong relationships with suppliers, I can offer high-quality products at competitive prices.

Q: How has this business impacted your life as a mom?

Lisa: It has been an incredible journey. Not only do I get to contribute financially to my family, but I also have the flexibility to be present for my kids. It's the perfect balance for me.

Chapter 3: Plant Nursery

For moms seeking a fulfilling and budget-friendly side hustle, a plant nursery emerges as an enchanting venture that blends passion with profit. Nestled within the nurturing embrace of nature, this green haven offers a tranquil escape where one can cultivate both beautiful flora and a thriving business. With an initial investment of just $100, this flourishing side hustle not only enriches lives but also blossoms into a source of joy and sustainable income for moms with a penchant for gardening and entrepreneurship.

A plant nursery, where growth seeds are planted and lovingly tended to, is a physical example of the miracles of motherhood. By taking care of a variety of floral gems, each bursting with distinct beauty and promise, this venture enables mothers to indulge their caring inclinations. Moms may create a calm paradise by cultivating and collecting a variety of plants, from colourful blooms to lush greenery, attracting both plant aficionados and others looking to spruce up their homes and gardens.

With an affordable startup cost of $100, moms can begin their journey into the world of plants, exploring the magic of propagation, gardening techniques, and plant care. As the nursery flourishes, the initial investment multiplies manifold, offering a rewarding and profitable return on passion and dedication.

A plant nursery allows moms to embrace the flexibility of a side hustle, tending to their plants with love while attending to family responsibilities. This balancing act infuses life with harmony, as the nurturing spirit extends from the home to the greenery that thrives under their care.

In this modern age, where sustainability and eco-consciousness are embraced wholeheartedly, a plant nursery finds its rightful place as a venture that nurtures not only plants but also a greener and more mindful lifestyle. As moms delve into this enchanting side hustle, they find themselves at the helm of a business that celebrates nature's abundance, embraces creativity, and fosters a community of fellow plant enthusiasts.

In this green sanctuary, moms discover the power of a $100 investment, transforming their passion for plants into a thriving side hustle that flourishes under the warmth of their love and dedication. With each leaf unfurling and each bloom unfurling, the journey of a plant nursery blooms into an enduring story of growth, beauty, and fulfillment.

The growing demand for personalized gift baskets and the opportunities in the gift-giving industry:

In recent years, there has been a remarkable rise in the popularity of gardening and the green movement, as individuals and communities around the world seek to connect with nature and embrace sustainable living. This growing interest in gardening and environmental consciousness has laid the foundation for a plant nursery to emerge as a highly viable and rewarding business idea.

- Embracing Nature in Urban Spaces: **As urbanization and modern living encroach upon green spaces, individuals are increasingly drawn to gardening as a way to reconnect with nature. In bustling cities, homes with limited outdoor spaces find solace in cultivating indoor plants and creating lush balconies or rooftop gardens. A plant nursery caters to this demand by offering a diverse range of indoor and urban-friendly plants that thrive in compact environments, allowing city dwellers to surround themselves with greenery and experience the therapeutic benefits of gardening.

- The Health and Wellness Connection: **The green movement's emphasis on health and wellness has led people to recognize the positive impact of plants on mental and physical well-being. Gardening is viewed as a calming and stress-relieving activity that promotes mindfulness and improves air quality. As people become more health-conscious, they seek out plant nurseries to bring nature into their homes and workspaces, creating an atmosphere of serenity and productivity.

- Sustainable Living and Eco-Consciousness: **The global focus on sustainability and eco-consciousness has driven individuals to adopt greener lifestyles. Plant nurseries play a pivotal role in supporting this movement by offering a wide variety of native plants, heirloom varieties, and organic gardening options. Customers are drawn to nurseries that prioritize sustainable practices, such as water conservation, recycling, and the use of eco-friendly materials.

- Growth of the "Plant Parent" Culture: **The rise of social media has given birth to the "plant parent" culture, where individuals proudly share their plant collections and experiences online. This digital community fosters enthusiasm for plants and gardening, inspiring others to become part of the green movement. Plant nurseries act as facilitators of this culture, providing an array of plant options and knowledge-sharing to support and nurture budding "plant parents."

- Demand for Unique and Rare Plants: **Gardening enthusiasts and collectors seek out plant nurseries for unique and rare plant species that are not readily available in conventional retail outlets. The allure of acquiring plants with intriguing foliage, vibrant blooms, or historical significance fuels the demand for specialized nurseries that cater to the diverse tastes of avid gardeners.

- Educational and Community Engagement: **Plant nurseries serve as educational hubs, offering workshops, seminars, and gardening events that empower individuals to hone their green thumbs. Community engagement through plant sales, gardening clubs, and charitable initiatives creates a sense of togetherness and fosters a shared passion for plants and the environment.

Chapter 4: Pet Services.

The pet services industry provides a warm and gratifying option for women looking for a lucrative and affordable financial venture. The need for skilled and compassionate pet services is rising as the link between pets and their owners gets closer. Moms may start a pet-focused business with a less than $100 investment, leveraging their love of animals and igniting their desire to give the best care possible.

Pet services encompass a wide array of offerings, from pet sitting and dog walking to grooming and training. As more individuals and families welcome pets into their homes, the demand for reliable, trustworthy, and personalized pet care services grows exponentially. For moms seeking flexibility and a chance to balance family life with a passion for animals, this business idea aligns perfectly, offering a chance to delve into a fulfilling side hustle or even scale it into a full-fledged enterprise.

The rise of the pet parent community has transformed the way we care for our furry companions. Pet owners are increasingly seeking personalized and attentive services for their beloved pets, ensuring they receive the love and care they deserve even in their absence. By venturing into the realm of pet services, moms have an opportunity to become an integral part of this nurturing community, providing a safe and welcoming haven for pets to thrive.

Low-Cost Entry with High Returns:

Starting a pet services business requires minimal financial investment, making it an accessible venture for moms looking to explore their entrepreneurial spirit on a budget. With less than $100, moms can acquire essential supplies, create promotional materials, and launch their pet services journey. As the business grows and gains recognition, the potential for higher returns and increased client referrals becomes a reality.

The various pet-related business opportunities, such as dog walking, pet sitting, and pet grooming.

1. Dog Walking:

Dog walking is a popular and essential pet-related service for busy pet owners who may not have enough time to take their dogs on regular walks. As a dog walker, you would be responsible for exercising and engaging the dogs in your care, ensuring they receive the physical activity they need to stay healthy and happy. This service is ideal for moms who enjoy spending time with dogs, as it allows them to combine their love for animals with outdoor activities and flexibility in their schedules.

2. Pet Sitting:

Pet sitting involves caring for pets in their owners' homes while they are away. As a pet sitter, you would be responsible for feeding, exercising, and providing companionship to the pets, ensuring they feel comfortable and secure in their familiar surroundings. This service is particularly appealing to moms who can offer a nurturing and loving environment for pets while their owners are on vacation or away for work.

3. <u>Pet Grooming</u>:

Pet grooming services involve bathing, brushing, trimming, and styling pets' fur, as well as cleaning their ears, trimming their nails, and maintaining their overall hygiene. As a pet groomer, you would help pets look and feel their best while also addressing any specific grooming needs they may have. This service requires a love for animals, attention to detail, and some grooming skills or training.

4. <u>Pet Boarding</u>:

Pet boarding services provide a temporary home for pets while their owners are away for an extended period. As a pet boarder, you would care for the pets in your own home or a designated facility, offering them a safe and comfortable environment with plenty of attention and care. This service is well-suited for moms who have the space and time to provide personalized care for pets.

5. <u>Pet Training</u>:

Pet training services involve teaching pets various commands, behaviors, and manners to improve their obedience and overall behavior. As a pet trainer, you would work with pet owners and their pets to address specific behavioral issues and instill positive habits. This service is ideal for moms who have experience or a passion for animal training and behavioral understanding.

6. Pet Photography:

Pet photography services cater to pet owners who want professional and memorable photographs of their beloved pets. As a pet photographer, you would capture the personality and essence of pets in various settings, creating cherished keepsakes for their owners. This service requires photography skills, creativity, and the ability to connect with animals to capture their best moments.

7. Pet Product Sales:

Pet product sales involve selling pet-related products, such as pet food, accessories, toys, grooming supplies, and more. As a pet product seller, you could operate an online store, a physical retail shop, or even participate in pet expos and events. This business opportunity allows moms to curate and offer products that align with their passion for pet care.

Each of these pet-related business opportunities offers a unique way for moms to combine their love for animals with a rewarding and fulfilling business venture. Whether it's taking dogs on invigorating walks, providing a safe and loving environment for pets, grooming them to look their best, or offering valuable pet-related products, there are countless ways for moms to embark on a successful and heartwarming pet-focused entrepreneurial journey.

Advice on building trust with pet owners and ensuring the safety and well-being of animals in your care.

Running a profitable and well-regarded pet-related business requires cultivating trust with pet owners and assuring the safety and welfare of the animals in your care. Here are some great pointers for achieving these objectives:

1. Professionalism and Clear Communication:

Maintain professionalism in all your interactions with pet owners. Be responsive to inquiries, provide clear information about your services, and establish transparent communication channels. Address any concerns or questions promptly and ensure that pet owners feel comfortable discussing their pet's specific needs with you.

2. Pet Health and Safety Measures:

Implement strict health and safety protocols to ensure the well-being of animals in your care. Make sure all pets are up-to-date on vaccinations and have received a thorough health check. Provide a safe and secure environment for pets, especially when they are in group settings, and monitor their behavior and interactions to prevent any potential issues.

3. Personalized Care Plans:

Create personalized care plans for each pet, taking into account their individual needs, preferences, and any medical considerations. Show genuine interest in understanding each pet's personality and habits, and be attentive to their emotional and physical well-being throughout their time in your care.

4. Build a Positive Reputation:

Deliver exceptional service consistently to build a positive reputation within the pet owner community. Encourage satisfied clients to leave reviews and testimonials, and share these on your website or social media platforms. Positive word-of-mouth recommendations can go a long way in establishing trust and attracting new clients.

5. Regular Updates and Photos:

Keep pet owners informed about their pets' activities and well-being while they are in your care. Send regular updates and photos to reassure them that their furry companions are happy, healthy, and enjoying their time with you. This level of communication helps build trust and provides peace of mind to pet owners.

6. Professional Pet Handling Skills:

Hone your pet handling skills to ensure the safety of both pets and yourself. Be aware of pet body language and respond appropriately to prevent any potential conflicts or accidents. Always handle pets with care and respect their boundaries.

7. Establish a Pet Owner Agreement:

Create a clear and comprehensive pet owner agreement that outlines the terms and conditions of your services, including care responsibilities, pricing, cancellation policies, and liability waivers.

Having a written agreement helps set clear expectations and protects both parties.

8. Invest in Pet Care Training:

Stay updated on best practices in pet care and consider investing in relevant training or certifications. Continuous learning will enhance your knowledge and expertise, demonstrating your commitment to providing the best care possible.

9. Insurance and Legal Protection:

Obtain appropriate insurance coverage for your pet-related business to protect yourself, your clients, and the pets in your care. This step ensures that you are prepared for any unforeseen circumstances and reinforces your commitment to professionalism and responsibility.

You may develop trusting connections with pet owners and develop a devoted clientele by placing a high priority on professionalism, safety, and individualised care. Gaining the confidence of pet owners is a sign of your commitment to offering first-rate pet care, turning your company into a sought-after source for pet owners in your neighbourhood.

Chapter 5: Subscription Box Service

This empowering business opportunity allows you to curate unique and exciting experiences for your subscribers, all while embracing your passion and celebrating your individuality.

Imagine the thrill of designing themed boxes that bring joy to the doorsteps of eager customers every month. With a subscription box service, you have the freedom to express your creativity, from handpicking high-quality products to designing captivating packaging that leaves a lasting impression. Your artistic flair and attention to detail will shine through, making your subscription boxes a true reflection of your vision and personality.

As a woman entrepreneur in this realm, you have the power to cater to a diverse audience, offering subscription boxes that cater to various interests and passions. Whether it's beauty and self-care, gourmet delights, home décor, or a delightful mix of surprises, the possibilities are boundless. Tailoring your offerings to meet the unique tastes of your subscribers will foster a loyal and engaged community that eagerly anticipates each new delivery.

Starting a subscription box service also enables you to embrace the modern world of e-commerce and digital marketing. With the ever-growing demand for online shopping and the convenience of subscription-based services, you can seize the opportunity to reach a global audience and make your mark on the digital landscape.

The flexibility of a subscription box business allows you to thrive at your own pace, fitting seamlessly into your lifestyle as a woman with varied responsibilities and aspirations. Whether it's a side hustle, a passion project, or a full-fledged venture, the power lies in your hands to shape your subscription box service into the perfect embodiment of your dreams.

Steps to Curate and Launch a Successful Subscription Box Service on a Budget:

Step 1: Define Your Niche and Target Audience:

Identify a specific niche for your subscription box service that aligns with your interests and expertise. Research your target audience to understand their preferences, needs, and pain points. A well-defined niche will help you curate a focused and appealing box that resonates with your potential subscribers.

Example: Let's say you are a passionate tea enthusiast who wants to curate a subscription box service centered around specialty teas. Your niche could be "Artisan Tea Delights," catering to tea connoisseurs and those seeking unique and flavorful tea experiences. Your target audience might include tea lovers who appreciate high-quality loose-leaf teas, herbal infusions, and delightful tea-related accessories.

Step 2: Source Affordable and High-Quality Products:

Look for suppliers and manufacturers that offer affordable yet high-quality products that fit your chosen niche. Consider negotiating bulk discounts and explore wholesale options to keep costs down. Prioritize unique and useful items that provide value to your subscribers.

Step 3: Set a Realistic Budget:

Establish a budget that outlines your expenses for product sourcing, packaging, shipping, and marketing. Be mindful of cost constraints and allocate funds wisely to ensure profitability. Starting small and gradually expanding your offerings can be a budget-friendly approach.

Step 4: Design Captivating Packaging:

Create eye-catching packaging that reflects your brand and the theme of your subscription box. Utilize cost-effective materials without compromising on presentation. A well-designed box enhances the unboxing experience and leaves a positive impression on your subscribers.

Step 5: Plan Your Subscription Model:

Decide on your subscription model, such as monthly, quarterly, or annual subscriptions. Consider offering discounts for longer commitments to incentivize longer-term subscriptions. Implement a user-friendly and secure payment system to streamline the subscription process.

Step 6: Launch a Minimal Viable Product (MVP):

Start with a minimum viable product that includes essential elements of your subscription box. This approach allows you to test the market with minimal investment and gather feedback from early subscribers. Use this feedback to improve and refine your box offerings.

Step 7: Build a User-Friendly Website:

Create a professional and user-friendly website to showcase your subscription box service. Use high-quality images and compelling copy to entice potential subscribers. Consider using a website builder platform to save on development costs.

Step 8: Implement Cost-Effective Marketing Strategies:

Utilize social media platforms, email marketing, and content marketing to promote your subscription box service. Engage with your target audience through captivating visuals, informative content, and customer testimonials. Leverage partnerships and collaborations with influencers or other small businesses to increase your reach without spending extensively on advertising.

Step 9: Offer Limited-Time Promotions:

Create a sense of urgency by offering limited-time promotions, discounts, or early-bird sign-ups. These tactics can drive initial sales and attract subscribers who are motivated by exclusive deals.

Step 10: Focus on Customer Experience:

Deliver exceptional customer service and prioritize the satisfaction of your subscribers. Respond promptly to inquiries and address any concerns or issues with care. A positive customer experience encourages word-of-mouth referrals and fosters long-term loyalty.

<u>Note</u>: You can create and operate a profitable subscription box service on a budget by adhering to these guidelines and using your creativity and resourcefulness. Keep in mind that starting small and expanding your business gradually will enable you to maintain your financial stability while providing your subscribers with a wonderful experience. Your inexpensive subscription box business can flourish and establish itself as a popular option in your target market with commitment, passion, and strategic planning.

Tips for Customer Retention:

- <u>Consistent Quality and Value</u>: Ensure that each subscription box delivers consistent quality and value to your subscribers. Avoid compromising on product selection and presentation, as maintaining high standards will build trust and encourage repeat subscriptions.
- <u>Personalization</u>: Tailor the subscription experience by allowing customers to customize their box contents or preferences. Consider offering surveys to gather feedback and understand their preferences better, leading to increased satisfaction and loyalty.
- <u>Surprise Gifts and Exclusive Offers</u>: Surprise subscribers with occasional bonus gifts or exclusive offers. Providing unexpected extras shows appreciation and incentivizes customers to stay subscribed.
- <u>Engaging Unboxing Experience</u>: Design an exciting and memorable unboxing experience for subscribers. Attention to packaging details, personalized notes, and creative inserts add a touch of excitement to each delivery.
- <u>Customer Feedback and Communication</u>: Listen to customer feedback, respond to inquiries promptly, and address any issues or concerns with empathy. Open and effective communication fosters a positive relationship with your subscribers.
- <u>Loyalty Rewards Program</u>: Implement a loyalty rewards program that offers incentives for long-term subscribers, such as discounts, free gifts, or early access to new themes.
- <u>Social Media and Community Engagement</u>: Cultivate a community around your subscription box service on social media. Engage with subscribers, encourage them to share their

unboxing experiences, and run contests or giveaways to foster interaction.

- <u>Referral Program</u>: Encourage subscribers to refer friends and family with a referral program. Offer discounts or rewards for successful referrals, expanding your subscriber base through word-of-mouth.
- <u>Post-Purchase Follow-Ups</u>: Send post-purchase follow-up emails to thank subscribers for their support and gather feedback on their experience. Use this information to make improvements and show that their satisfaction is your priority.

Creative Themes to Keep Subscribers Engaged:

- <u>Seasonal Delights</u>: Curate boxes that embrace the flavors and colors of each season. For example, a "Spring Awakening" box could feature light and floral teas, while a "Cozy Winter Warmers" box could include rich hot cocoa blends.
- <u>Around the World</u>: Explore teas and treats from different regions or cultures. Feature teas from India, matcha from Japan, and biscuits from England to take subscribers on a global taste adventure.
- <u>Wellness Retreat</u>: Focus on self-care and wellness with a box containing soothing herbal teas, relaxation products, and mindfulness tools.
- <u>Tea and Books</u>: Pair specialty teas with a carefully chosen book that complements the tea's theme or origins. This theme appeals to book lovers who enjoy a cozy reading experience with a cup of tea.

- <u>Tea Party Celebration</u>: Create a festive box suitable for hosting a tea party. Include tea accessories, tea sandwiches recipes, and elegant tableware for an unforgettable tea gathering.
- <u>Flavor Fusion</u>: Introduce innovative flavor combinations by blending teas with unexpected ingredients like fruits, spices, or even edible flowers.
- <u>Garden-to-Cup</u>: Feature teas made from ingredients sourced directly from local gardens or small-scale farms, showcasing the essence of freshness and sustainability.
- <u>Tea and Art</u>: Collaborate with local artists to design exclusive packaging or include art prints inspired by the tea's theme.

YOU
CAN
DO IT!